NEWSLETTER BONUS

Sign up to our free newsletter at **ColorfulCalm.com**

You will receive free coloring pages, information on our latest book releases, as well as a chance to win free coloring supplies.

Thank you for purchasing this coloring book and enjoy learning how to swear around the world!

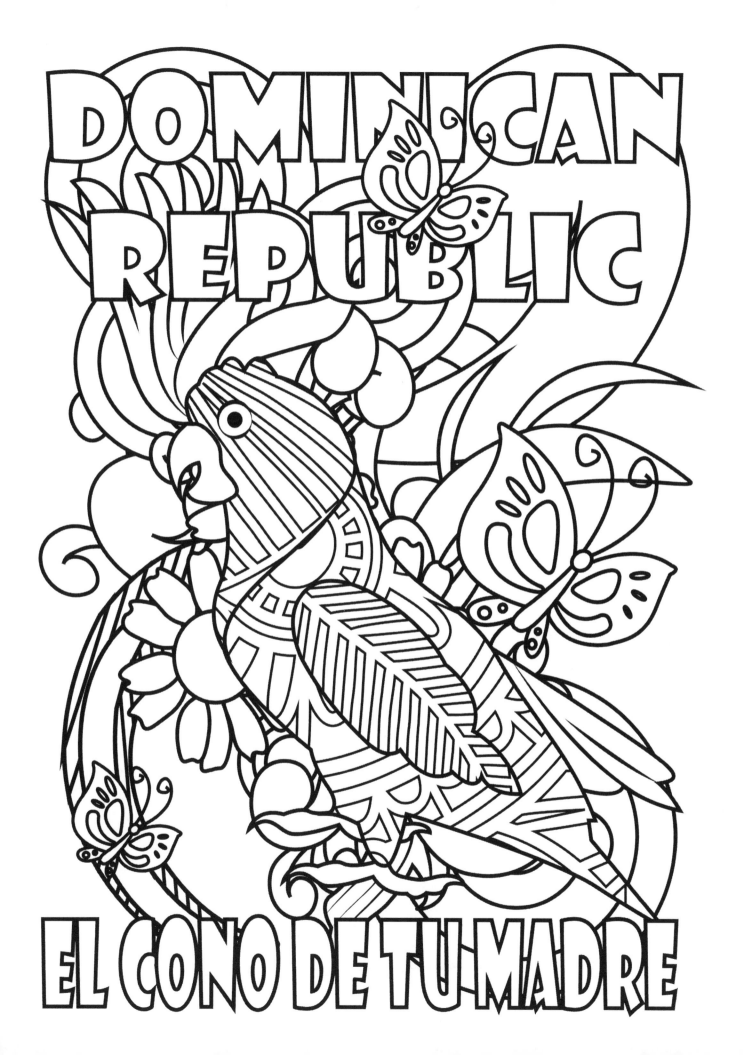

India

Ku Gihen

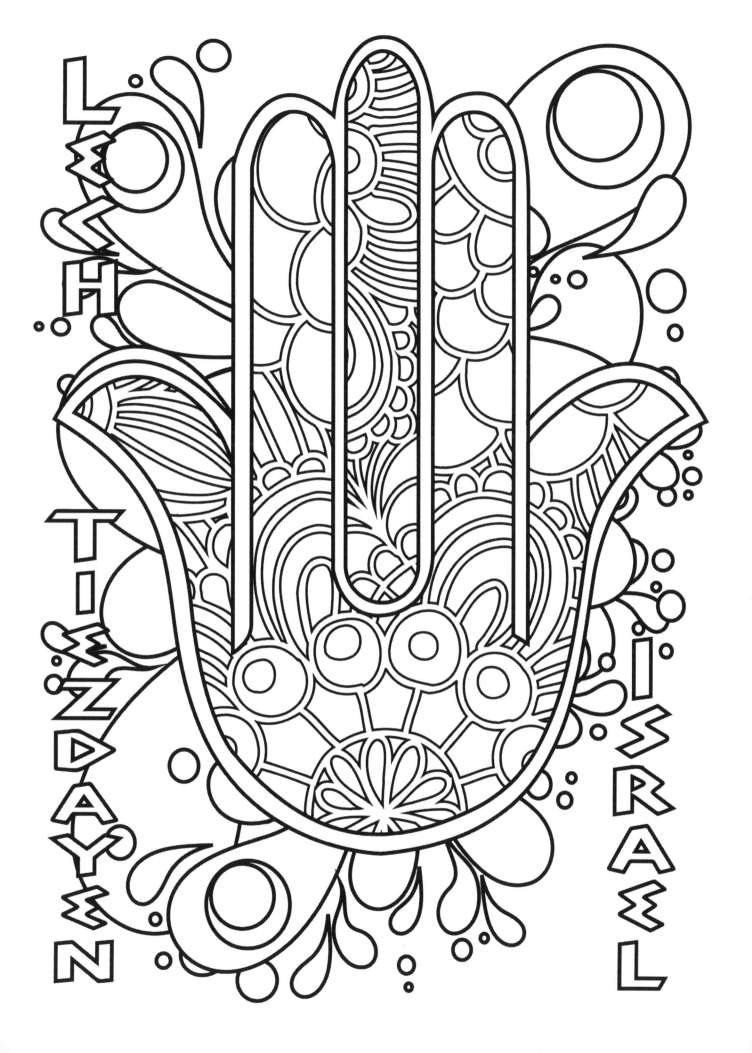

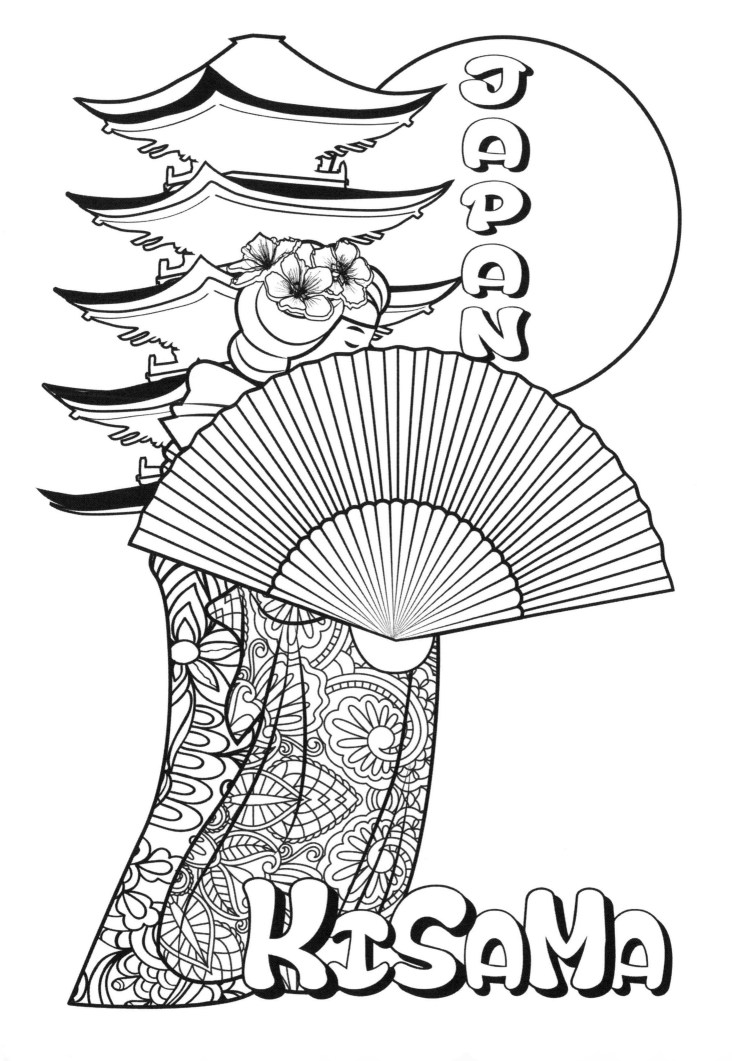